The House of Being

The House of Being

Poems of Humanity and Nature

Winner of The Local Legend National
Spiritual Writing Competition

PETER WALKER

Peter Walker © 2018

All rights reserved

No parts of this publication may be reproduced, stored in a retrieval system, or transmitted in any form or by any means whatsoever without the prior permission of the publisher.

A record of this publication is available from the British Library.

ISBN: 978-1-910027-26-4

Typesetting by Wordzworth Ltd
www.wordzworth.com

Cover design by Titanium Design Ltd
www.titaniumdesign.co.uk

Printed by Lightning Source UK
www.lightningsource.com

Cover image by the author

Published by Local Legend
www.local-legend.co.uk

About the Author

Peter Walker is a teacher, priest and poet.

After graduating in French and Philosophy, he taught languages for many years while at the same time trained for the priesthood. "It was in the wee small hours," he says, "as I looked after our baby daughter that I came to experience the over-arching love of God holding all things together." He was ordained in the Church of England and for the last few years has been a Team Vicar in the Church in Wales.

Peter has written poetry since his teenage years but his recent work reflects in particular his Welsh experiences and his interest in Celtic spirituality. He is much influenced by both the natural world ("... in the way it provides glimpses of the divine unity of all things") and the way in which our human experiences are mediated by language.

Yet Peter is nonetheless down-to-earth, loving "red wine and strong coffee, the vibrancy of the inner city and the deserted shoreline at dawn, the music of Muddy Waters and of Vaughan Williams."

He has led poetry retreats and quiet days, and is married to Susie, with whom he has a daughter.

Previous collections of poetry

Penmon Point	ISBN: 978-1847713698 (2011)
Old Men in Jeans	ISBN: 978-1847714343 (2012)
Listening to Zappa	ISBN: 978-1847717030 (2013)
A Pocketful of Myrrh	ISBN: 978-1784611415 (2015)

Published by Y Lolfa, Tal-y-bont, Ceredigion, Mid-Wales

Contents

PART ONE	1
There is a Space	2
Reading the Creed	3
The House of Being	4
Learning to Dance	5
Too Many Words	6
My Mother's Diary	7
We are Afraid of Silence	8
Liverpool	9
Open Mic	10
OMG	12
My Beard	13
Gerry does Elvis	14
Coleg y Groes, Corwen	16
Battalion Colours	17
Pilkem Ridge	18
Body	19
Sixty-Five	20
Quiet Days	22
Advent	24
Prayer	25
Strange	26
The Waiting Time	28
The Llangystennin Bell	29
Naming	30

My Burying Shoes	32
Why I Go To Church	33
Same River Once	34
PART TWO	**37**
St Giles	38
As the Bud ...	39
Driving	40
Magpies	42
Bee	44
February	45
Sea and Rain	46
Night Rain	47
Hills	48
Noddfa	49
Penmaenmawr	50
Why I Hate Mushrooms	51
The Tide at Aberdyfi	52
Michaelmas	53
Three Haiku	54
Never	55
Holy Spirit	56
Low Tide	57
Well-Hunting	58
Ynys Seiriol	59
Sunflower on the Motorway	60
The Sky is Beautiful	61

Part One

There is a Space

there is a space within me

sometimes it feels as if it has been
scooped and hollowed out by God
who waits patiently for the invitation
and then
like a cat
will curl up on the hearth of my heart

sometimes it feels as if it has been
chipped and mined and the black coal hauled
so that God can fill it with grace and benediction

sometimes it feels as if it has been
ripped out of me by life's wild horses
and God has nothing to do with it
but by implication
for the part torn out of me
is you

Reading the Creed

what is non-negotiable?

despite the fervour
and the clamour
and the ache for certainty
the quest for orthodoxy
and the damning of the contrary
the claims of those who claim authority
who read and know
and tell me what I should believe
there is an ocean of love only
that bears mercy
should I be brave enough to cast off
ragged rules

The House of Being

"Language is the house of Being"
–MARTIN HEIDEGGER, LETTER ON HUMANISM

I am my own myth
I invent myself with preterites

    a little to the north
    of the jaundiced moon in its shawl of cloud
    the rain shuffles in with coat and scarf
    and shakes its drizzled head across the panes

as I find my voice I lose it again
my soul is in my words
and when they fall silent where am I?

    like scattered ash strewn across a fresh-ploughed field
    the high wind pricks the eyes to tears

the concept lies in the space between
and the space between is intuition
and intuition is founded on the dictionary of my aching heart

    moment by moment there is no sense of time
    only reruns and the goal beyond
    the fear of resurrection:
    word, concept, myth:
    as if anything mattered other than vocabulary

we spend our time becoming
and forget to be

Learning to Dance

one foot anchored on the firm, damp sand
one foot tapping out the time
in the sun-hot ripples of the waves

one hand holding tight on rope or stave
one hand reaching up into that glorious emptiness
of self-abandonment

caught between the now I know
and that uncertainty that makes me who I am
I invent the choreography of life

Too Many Words

from the first bloomed rose
perceived in consciousness
we stare
agog
across the endless procession
of homoousios*
at new-hatched rhymes
megastars and gigabytes
cool or random
buff or sick
at those who play with words
drooling over their rich meanderings
some Eliot pounding on the keys
flaunting fame and Faber

and yet we long to bathe again in
Mallarmé's sparse vowels
to narrow the vision
like sun's energy trapped within a lens
and focus on the cataract that dims us
and in that beam to realise
there is only one Word
that echoes round
the hollow space between our bones

Greek: all things are of the same essence

My Mother's Diary

In memoriam Dorothy Walker, 1923-2018

each year my mother took her new
thin diary
week to view
and in her increasingly spidery hand
copied up the dates from the year before

family ages
one year added
marriage and divorce
the family litany of birthdays
of aunts and uncles and cousins and their brood
and friends

"Rita will be 95 this year – well I never!"
and then the tales of an unrecognisable land
of lard and tripe and gutting hens
of searchlights and waiting and waitresses in pubs
of love and romance as if just yesterday

"Flo would have been 98 this month –
I miss her so … the dinners and the stories
and the people that she knew"

and then the roll-call of the dead
fourteen years since …
two years since …
and this day fifty years ago …

and so it goes
each white page another funeral stone
that grows grey with cataracts and time

but no more of that now
I have another date to add to my own
thin diary
if I can bear to raise the pen

We are Afraid of Silence

    we are afraid of silence

the agonised silence of the cross
and the silence of God in that hanging

    we are afraid of silence

the silence of the space after our prayerful call
and the silence of our own voice inarticulate

    we are afraid of silence

the silence of the empty room of our grief
and the silence of those who fear their own tongue

    we are afraid of silence

the silence of a complicit world before its own pain
and the silence of those who turn away

    we are afraid of silence

the silence of the dark soul-night
and the silence of the answer that returns in that darkness

    we are afraid of silence

Liverpool

A city seen as a parable

living on hope
around the corner from Everyman
waking to a crown of
stainless steel thorns
framed by blue sky curtains
then
walking away
yet
walking towards
the squat
square
visible
and cruciform

wherever I run
you search me out

Open Mic

I start with my voice a tone higher than my normal voice
and then I modulate along the line
dropping my voice in the middle
before I raise it at the end
and
if I can
I put on a mild Liverpool accent
because then I sound a bit like Roger McGough
whom I really like
a lot

T S Eliot I pretend to like
but really I have no idea what he's on about
and the rest are very old or very dead
or
let's face it
very old and very dead
and so I resort to the dictionary to find words
redolent with perspicacity
and with a meniscus of semiotic Marxist undertow

and it's always good to put in the occasional "shit"
to get a laugh

and the sentence weaves its way
    through endless subordinate clauses
which in themselves are quite acceptable
but piled on top of one another
which they are
lest you miss the subtlety of the point I try to make
with its references to mystic Avalon
and far-flung realms where I may have been
(or maybe I just imagined it)
would make an academic yawn
nay sleep
and now I think I've lost the plot
oh shit
there it is again

quit while you're ahead

OMG

God likes me
He ticked me on Facebook
and wants to be my friend

but I don't trust Him
`cause I've read His blog

He says He loves us but then
He is selective in whom He helps and heals
He answers prayers haphazardly
perhaps
and speaks ironically

before the timeless became measured
as ancient and modern
He was post-modern

I follow His Son on Twitter
#HairyLunatic
`though that may be ironic too

"they're coming to get me
can't say any more
see you in three days
if you know what I mean"

I prefer to sit and wait
and when my iPhone pings
I'll know it's the Holy Spirit
and I'll be off to that party
in a flash

honest

... come on, ping

My Beard

I am not a trendsetter

I duly ape the fashionistas
two steps behind
in a playground dance
follow-my-leader

an earring at thirty or so
and a tattoo at forty
blue 501s while those around me
are wearing black

and now I forego the soap and scrape
and watch the grey crumbs lengthen on cheek and chin
but in the mirror I am
not so much rugged as care-worn
a scruffy old tramp
who should know better

Mr Potato-Head with blight
which
I guess
is all I am

Gerry does Elvis

** insert expletive of your choice

    My mate Gerry
is a dosser on the dole
he's a tosser on the dole
(and he's not that ** old)
    My mate Gerry
is a dosser on the dole
and he thinks he's Elvis Presley
    (which he ain't)

    My mate Gerry
was a bugger when at school
he broke every ** rule
but was never downright cruel
    My mate Gerry
was a bugger when at school
and acted like Elvis Presley
    (or thought he did)

    My mate Gerry
worked at Rover all his life
divorced wife and wife and wife
'til redundancy's cold knife
    My mate Gerry
worked at Rover all his life
and sneered like Elvis Presley
    (well, he tried to)

    My mate Gerry
born with a ** quiff
uses gel to keep it stiff
grew sideburns, liked a spliff
    My mate Gerry
born with a ** quiff
and looked like Elvis Presley
    (in his dreams)

    My mate Gerry
dresses like a Ted
dyes the hair upon his head
sleeps in a single bed
    My mate Gerry
dresses like a Ted
to look like Elvis Presley
    (in the `50s)

    My mate Gerry
could have sung in clubs
sings Elvis overdubs
in karaoke pubs
    My mate Gerry
could have sung in clubs
and been like Elvis Presley
    (his pals say)

    My mate Gerry
had a coronary last night
he went up to take a shite
in the glaring bathroom light
    My mate Gerry
had a coronary last night
and he died like Elvis Presley
    (which he did)

Coleg y Groes, Corwen

where shall we sleep tonight and when do we go
we are pawing the rug of our mortality
will I be in time for Corwen

... the calm and peace
with the river sparkling
beneath the rocking chair moon
and the last of the autumn leaves hanging
hanging

the curious and the challenged
our conversation went something like
if the ministry is right
can the place be wrong

musings
hopping like rabbits
for the music of our souls
is the framework of our being

Corwen is a small Welsh town near Llangollen. Seven of us met here at the Coleg y Groes for a day of reflection and writing.

Battalion Colours

for a Passchendaele Memorial Service

if that far field were not grown gold with wheat
we would see rags of grey and khaki cloth
caught on pins of rusted iron

if that far slope were not green with grass
we would see scarlet trails
imagine ashen faces
lit by cordite flares

if this good earth were not ploughed
rich and brown
we might till the twisted
blunted steel of shell
and harrow the muddied copper of a cartridge case

if all this place were not chalked with line on line of stone
we might pass the poppies by
red as veins
and wonder how we ever learned to sing of peace
in robes of white
and lay the colours down like men in silent prayer

Passchendaele was one of the bloodiest battles of World War One and memorial services were held in 2017 to mark its centenary and to remember the sacrifice and courage of those who took part.

Pilkem Ridge

where was God at Passchendaele?
    in the mud, in the mud
where was God when courage failed?
    in the mud, in the mud

where was God on Pilkem Ridge?
    in the mud, in the mud
where was God in shell-hole ditch?
    in the mud, in the mud

where was God for my pal Joe?
    in the mud, in the mud
where was God for all our foes?
    in the mud, in the mud

where is God at trumpet call?
    on the wall, on the wall
where is God in marble halls?
    on the wall, on the wall

where is God when war's recalled?
    on the wall, on the wall
where is God when names are called?
    on the wall, on the wall

where is God when poppies fall?
    on the wall, on the wall
where is God in churches all?
    on the wall, on the wall

Body

"This is my body."

this flat
insipid
skin-thin discus
lifeless
cold
tossed like a coin
pre-moulded icon
we break ... nothing
we share ... nothing
we feel ... nothing
and we know ... nothing

and yet

"This, too, is my body."

rounded
fleshed
pierced through layers of muscle
cooling
limp
hung like beef
blood dripping
we break ... you
we share ... you
we feel ... you
and we know ... ourselves

Sixty-Five

For Louise

sixty-fucking-five thy father lies
an OAP to the DWP
and those are tears that were his eyes

though nineteen in my head
innocent and unloved
shaggy beard
shaggy clothes
shaggy life
but now
with hope of eternity and fear of oblivion

so when I'm dribbling
gaga
stick me in a corner
with a bag of weed and a subscription to lesbian porn
and let me hazily drift away

Φ

musing:
    oh God let the world be run by women
    with their nurture and growth and loving the lost
    but let it not be run by feminists
    with their preening and demeaning and bemoaning their lot

musing:
    I think the world will drown in coffee pods
    even though I spend my life in Costa queues
    waiting for the next latte
    and outside the world passes me by

musing:
    the council is on strike again
    the park bins filled with multi-coloured balloons of dog-shit
    bags
    like a display of bulbous plastic flowers
    pink and green and blue and black
    a fetid rainbow of creatureliness
    that brings us back full-circle to our own sad bodies

musing:
    and are we come to this
    a cross of ash spread in a garden
    while words of hope are said

Φ

at least there are those words
and all that they invoke

and the saddest thing of all my dear
is
this is not forever
this is not
this is
this
this
this
and only this

Quiet Days

food for quiet days:
crisps
Cox's apples when the juice runs free
celery dusted with salt
cucumber thick on crusty bread
paper bags of pear drops
ready for the crunch
clinking china cups

I wish to still my voice
but not my soul

Φ

not in weasel words
the drooping lids
of afternoon somnolence
the idle chatter after justice
and point-scoring tempest of indignation
not even in the endless
sentences of contemplation
the stuttering recitation of crafted lines
or the chiselled hour of silence

but in
the space between them all
before the chalice
touches lips
the catch of eye
and I am seen

Φ

notes tell me what I thought back then:
walk more
more wine
and now the voices say
be quiet
because these are not holy thoughts
not sanctified by authority
too prosaic
too worldly

but come
I hear
what do you want?

and I shall put on sturdy shoes
and brave the wind
that whips the spray and sand
and sip rich port
remembering

Advent

seven signs have brought us here
to reflect
on our diminishing

once I saw stars that presaged wings and wonder
took time to hear the stories of the lost
felt others' pain and shed long tears for them
touched hands that trembled with pain or loss
I loved without a care
that love would have to stand the test of time
and last beyond the bitter ditch
and laughed the endless joy that heaven knows

and now I have to slough the skin of time's sad sorrow
the mean emotions that cake my soul with grime
unlearn to see the world as others see it
to hear my own voice speak certainties
to laugh at misery
to touch my own raw wounds
and long for you to cry and feel my hurt

and there is hope in this
that in the renewal of our story
we too may be born again
in some sad stall
where angels gather to proclaim
the wonder
of our flourishing

Prayer

in the silence
there is silence

in the listening
there is listening

in the mutuality of consciousness
there is consciousness
turning with the spheres

the pin-prick violent stars
become mere holes of violet light
in the vast and velvet curtain
of infinity

words drip like water
on the limestone slab of cold indifference
and slowly etch a hollow
for our tears

Strange

strange eyes
looking past and through
as opaque to my being as I am transparent
skinless to them
a film to an inner world
if they were looking at the stars they would see themselves
at the far left field of vision
hazed and haloed
like a lamp in mist

strange sounds
from an inner room where I dare not go
literal and metaphoric
a history that speaks its battles now
that calls in pain of loss
and limitation
of small demands that grow to wound
or soundless mouthings of a mute brain
that will not let its frustrated words
call in joy or sorrow
but taps them out in semaphore
along the keypad of our frantic yearnings

strange bodies
twisted out of shape
cushioned and swaddled like coddled eggs
racked on a slim bed while the TV plays inconsequences
hands bent on themselves
as if to grip a barely life
that seeks to touch itself and know it's real
pushed and pulled and washed and treasured
held in puzzled compassion

strange God
that leaves perfection as a mirrored tool
that knows imperfectly the limitations of its powers
that looks impassively on its own flawed creatures
that lets them suffer in a world that makes itself
for there is no making without a womb of pain
beauty is not beautiful alone

we worship the scarred and wounded
for then we learn the truth that leads us home
that God Himself requires our fallen world
before He can see the icy stillness
of His own trapped being

The Waiting Time

advent is a time of waiting
waiting
for birth ...
life ...
growth ...
death ...
birth ...
a ceaseless helix of
mere waiting

shoddy and unkempt as
half-cut lines

PETER WALKER

The Llangystennin Bell

A 9th century Celtic bell is on display in Llandudno museum

from now to then
half-way in our counting
this hollow
blackened ingot
is the fulcrum of our prayers
that lie balanced
between eternities

a thousand years of yearning
in this empty bowl
that longs for filling
an aching heart
that tolls its desire for fullness
for flourishing
for renewal
in each broken soul

Naming

they brought creatures for him to name
and he named them
in accordance with his will

snake serpent schlange
cow vache buwch
horse pferd ceffyl
chat katze cath

and in the naming he thought he tamed them
but their wild wind freedom hid inside
and volcanoed out with the first sniff of spring
and so he gave the names of demons to their strivings
as if the naming would push them deep within
and hold them caged and collared
but it was not to be

and so it was with other creatures
that haunted the night sweats
he named them the devil's children
the swellings and the pox
the falling sickness
and the red weals around an open wound
that blackened and greened and stank and led to death

and death itself
was named in many ways
and mocked through fear
and yet it too was wild and free
and struck with a ripping claw

and even with dissections and the microscope
as enlightenment is born and born again
even the Latinisation of our crawling
faulty genes
does not mean that he can tame
the cancers that sidle up to him
unaware
and nip his throat and bowel

he blames those who brought these creatures
for he thinks that names are power
yet
he too is named

he is not tamed

My Burying Shoes

today
I put on my burying shoes
again
and walked the sodden sod in slow
slow time
to the bricked grave
I slipped and slithered in the sticky sludge
and stood on the chiselled edge of infinity
with its soft pillow of leaves
that would soften the launch of the sad barque
on its last voyage

I played my part in the ambivalent ritual
and wondered if
by constant repetition
the words would take meaning and make sense
or if they would remain as hollow and empty
as the cold
damp air

at home
I scraped off the caked mud
that fell like ash
dry and dusty
and polished away the smell of earth
knowing that I would have to walk
that same slow walk
another day and another
until someone walks it
then for me

Why I Go To Church

well
it's something that I do
it's my turn for the coffee
and to meet my friends
catch up on gossip
to sing aloud
to sing within
to give a shape to life

my neighbour brought me
or my neighbour asked me to bring him/her
but I forgot last week
to glorify the Lord
I wanted to
I thought I would

but my friend died last week

to hear our banns
to pray for those poor people in …
because I'm angry with myself
and angry too with God
because I wonder
because I wonder why
to touch the cloak of Christ

to touch another human hand

Same River Once

All is flux – you cannot step into the same river twice.
What you mean is, you cannot step into the same river once!

you cannot step
you cannot step into the same river
you cannot step into the same
you cannot step into the same river once
you cannot step into
you cannot
you

Φ

there are many stories
but they say
there are really only two
a going and a coming
departure and arrival
pilgrim and stranger
and therein lies all the incarnation

but then they say
there's really only one story:
who am I?

what was
what is
what is to come
inconstant construct of the words we speak

Φ

the smooth stone
is worn to its dusty roundness
by the ragged waves
and the rolling thunder of their breaking
the high winter tides running in
beneath the purple of the black-west sky

the sharp and jagged flinty shale
dug from beneath the barren patch
that would not yield to brassica or rose
lies heavy on the edge of its oblivion
sullen in its bold and spiked aggression

yet this too
if we took the time to tumble it
would be plundered by the to and fro
and in that milling
become bran and husk and germ

when is the rock itself?

does each grain of sand
retain the imprint of what it was
or can each granite slab
imagine its own powdery demise

in the pounding
does it become what it should be
or
does it lose the roughness of its soul

Φ

you cannot step into the same river
once

Part Two

St Giles

walking down St Giles
I was touched
by the first brown finger
of an autumn hand
from nowhere
from a beech that kept its distance
under the blue
high warmth

it was a cold, prescient hand
that rested on my shoulder
and made me stop and pluck it off
but the pondering of it
left its dusty print of veins across my soul

As the Bud...

as the bud
senses the coming warmth
and gently unfolds itself
uncurling
fingers
gripped tight upon themselves
against the cold
opening its dusty butterfly wing
and baring its speckled heart
so it stands tall
and drinks in life

Driving

I have travelled to the moon and back
across the vast black deep of years
from seventeen
and through the century's gate

I have ridden high
to the white-tipped waves of Pyrenees
and down the scree of Idris
to the valley floor
waded through the slop and gurgle
of the Sargasso sea of heavy traffic
brushed up against
the sperm-whale juggernaut
that hid the sun

I have seen monsters and wrecked hulks
rusted with blood
held hands of lost and dying souls
and gathered up the bleached and broken bones
of broken lives
cast upon the shore

this peregrination
in Brendan's wake
to coracle the Severn vale
to scull the Thames
to drift
where wind and wave and breath of God
pull and push
to discern the current
sometimes with and then against
to tack and seek the Spirit's gust

for we are pilgrims
in the pin-prick night
navigating by a cross-wire compass
seeking a lagoon
of love

Magpies

wood pigeon
tumbling
helter skelter
playing in the thermals
demi-semi-quavers
racing against staves of cirrus
then stiffening
spitfire-winged
to glide into glissando
a stretched and single note
against the harmony of cuckoo-calls
and blackbird arpeggio
while swallows
pick pizzicato
in the blue dome

F major 7th
the chord of Pentecost

rooks
like a Paganini score
dipping and swirling
with mad eyes
fuelled by pterodactyl brain
chasing magpies from their swampy green
while their wings dance tunes
their one Jurassic note
is played out to crescendo
in a thousand throats
until the air
is filled to boiling with their bubbly breath

and my one voice is joined with theirs
hoping that the volume of our prayers
will chase the magpies of my fears
away

Bee

mid-afternoon
heavy boughs droop
weary
need a lift of air
to raise their corn-dust leaves

siesta stillness

dry cough of a solitary rook
in the leathern beech
disturbed by pigeon flutter

one languid bee
flicks
finicky
from stem to bending stem
caresses clover cup
and rubs the pollen
in a slow
lubricious dance
along its belly
and ignores
the splayed and butter heart
of wanton daisy

February

turbines are turning
above Ynyslas

the toy boat
of supermarket cartons and plastic bags
is abandoned
dry
washed up upon the shore
and waits the turning tide

north wind blows cool
the western sun is summer warm
five figures cross the sand
in two and two and one
shaking off the long drab winter

golden flowers of gorse
burst from green thorns
dead trees grow buds

and Easter is but a dream
of pain away

Sea and Rain

a ghost of mist
erases the horizon
with a rub of chalk

cod-skin
scales a-shimmer
in the shiver shower rush

inscrutable and unmoving
alabaster Buddha face
a hint of tide
slow breath
of mantra meditation
absorbing

rattle of stone and dive of mullet
sunken drum and roll of clam
bottle glass and waving wrack

all melted
into soup of story
how we are
and were
and will yet be

all this
beneath the stillness
of an inner gaze

Night Rain

the soft touch of waking rain
stippling roof and window pane
in the rattling hours

the jangled doppelgänger
of the soul's night
dappling dreams and horses
in the pitter-pat

the shudder and heart-skip of fear
at the whispered rustling
across the dampening grass

wispy whiskery wisdom
brushes back the grey fronds of mist
to spittle weasel words of sly comfort

thank God for light
that drags us
sullenly
to spiteful consciousness

Hills

I set out early
my rucksack on my back
the hoar-frost
on the twisted branches of the apple trees
dipped in yellow sun
dripped cold
clear drops on me

beyond each green hill that I climbed
another one would offer
the open palm of its valley
as an invitation

I let the weight of the pack go
and saw it tumble down the steep scree
and I was light as the high air
where the red kites planed

and then another peak
pure with spring snow
and another still
until the one I left came round again

and I saw with different eyes
the empty path that
asked me to touch it
with my dusty boots

Noddfa

the stretch of sea
from Ynys Mon to Pen y Gogarth
a lap of gull-wing
frosted dawn
a hint of Turkish silk
shot with shamrock
a froth of cloud above
a balm of ice
to cool and call to rest
a bath of silence
stirring
stirring

Penmaenmawr

tumbled scree
upon gouged mountain face
slate scar pock holes
deserted desert
a passion of paths
criss-cross the waste and dross

bleak blackness
squirrel-grey
casting dark shadows
across the capricious sun
reminds us yet of how we mine
our long inheritance
and seek to shelter
in creation's arms

and how the thing we love
we sometimes crucify

Why I Hate Mushrooms

the modest parasol of sun-kissed dawn
that springs unbidden
from beneath the yew tree
opens with the light its cloak of fawn
and lifts its skirts to paddle in the dew

but stinkhorn
sulphur tuft and chanterelle
the inkcap
and the agaric and all
with velvet skin that folds
like veiny gill
and hold the spores that drop like seeds of gall

the smell that rises from their flesh of grey
is odour from the cemetery floor
or from the mortuary technician's
bowl of clay
that moulds itself to orifice and pore

the fungoid forms stalk out like death's dark wave
and leak with the putrescence
of the grave

The Tide at Aberdyfi

the inconsequential advance of
tide
imperceptibly
pirouettes past anchored sloop
and whispers to a jetty stanchion
hiding its true depth

its eddies and its ridged banks
of eel-grass
will
at its height
turn tail
and shrink back towards red west
as surely as the breath
that echoes and re-echoes in the lungs
and is the sea that flows
in all of us

Michaelmas

the late September evening sun
sinking low past Penmaenbach
leaks memory of spring
to dancing midges
freshly hatched
hovering in spotlight yolk
translucent rainbow wings
that rise and fall
barometers of angel dust
and fade invisible
within a cape of shade

Three Haiku

rain falling on waves
each drop blending into sea
today I am zen

mist over mountains
masking owl and hunting moon
mussel boat passes

today I am zen
each tear blending into sea
rain falling on waves

Never

I will never learn to love
these blue fields
with their stiff-necked
long-nosed sheep

the stone walls that come
right to the road's edge
as if the soil itself
wished to hide its thin pale body

the grey slate blackened by the rain
that turns the hills
to sheets of steel
expressionless

and then the flat terrace of the sea
beneath the sun
to warm the saints
that are almost tangible
almost …
almost …

Holy Spirit

I am reborn
ever young
each new keble morning
untouched pearl of dew
around a grit of brokenness

I flex my wings
dust-dried feathers
spread wide
to embrace the parabola of sky
I dive in blue

I rise and fall
barometer of parables
drawing curtains
on a frost-crisp dawn

oh happy days
as bodies fail and sink
I am the child
that sucks on heaven's milk
that takes a faltering step
that learns to spell out love
that wakes in each of us
if we but stopped to hear

as each day darkens
ever young
to light
I am reborn

Low Tide

snail-trail memories of spume
soft-jog soles
dip and weave
of excited black-and-tan
here a leap
there a pirouette
scattered pellets of a shot of flies
among the sea-wrack
and
behind it all
the constant susurrus
inescapable
yet
tuned out by intimacy
that will wash clean
the bones of this fair day

Well-Hunting

marked out
across the landscape of our faith
each small water-hole
of pilgrimage

and so we search
dry throat
husky with need
we prod the empty grave space
for a hint of leakage
look for tumbled walls long-brambled
and long-since pillaged for their heavy bounty
delve the ancient maps
question sages in their ancient homes

they told me once ...
we used to play ...
the rain collects in ...
Bryn Fynnon here ...
there Bron y Nant ...

and we slake our thirst in questing
and fill out gullets
with the wine of hope
and pray that if we strike the rock
there will be other deserts
through which our nomad hearts can tramp

Ynys Seiriol

I stepped out resenting smallness
bemoaning wasted time
I'd spent in groups of twos or threes
when surely there should be greater things

but then
beneath the grey sky
above grey sea
the low shore of Môn a charcoal smudge
upon the retina
the sun picked out the halo of that place
corn-yellow
close enough to touch the luminescence
of the shore
and the bright-green haunt of plovers' wings

I am my hermitage
and two or three should be enough
for we are called
to do the little things

Sunflower on the Motorway

between
entrances and exits
cool washed morning and grime evening
Apollinaire's beheading and dragon purple

on the central reservation
between
lines of traffic
refusing the protection of dull grey rivets
grows
a jagged
fragile halo

echoes of Van Gogh
lavender dawns
hovering hawk afternoons
melon-pipped
epiphany of light

yet
full throttle takes us past
with just a glimpse
and then
it is October

The Sky is Beautiful

the sky is beautiful
and yet ...
'sky' is a construct
we surmise
for the emptiness before us

you are beautiful
and yet ...
'you' is a construct
we invent
for the alien other

the world is beautiful
and yet ...
'world' is a construct
that encompasses pain
and death and misery

God is a construct
and yet ...

If you have enjoyed this book...

Local Legend is committed to publishing the very best spiritual writing, both fiction and non-fiction. You might also enjoy:

A MESSAGE FROM SOURCE
Grace Gabriella Puskas (ISBN 978-1-910027-00-4)

This debut collection of inspirational spiritual poetry was a previous winner of the Local Legend national Spiritual Writing Competition. Every so often, though rarely, a very special new voice is heard in the world. It does not shout. It does not need to use pompous phrases or bad language to get your attention. At first, you may not even realise that it has spoken to you. But once its words have entered your mind, they reach deep within your consciousness. And you are changed, your outlook on life different. This is such a voice.

AURA CHILD
A I Kaymen (ISBN 978-1-907203-71-8)

One of the most astonishing books ever written, telling the true story of a genuine Indigo child. Genevieve grew up in a normal London family but from an early age realised that she had very special spiritual and psychic gifts. She saw the energy fields around living things, read people's thoughts and even found herself slipping through time, able to converse with the spirits of those who had lived in her neighbourhood. This is an uplifting and inspiring book for what it tells us about the nature of our minds.

ONE PAIR OF SHOES
Mollie Peace (ISBN 978-1-907203-39-8)

Mollie Peace was a woman of her time, one of a generation that saw the most extraordinary changes. Born in poverty, she lived through the hardship (and some joys) of the early twentieth century, and experienced the tragedies of war. She witnessed the birth of the motor car, the atom bomb, the computer and the Internet. A loyal wife and mother, she raised a family and saw the birth of great-grandchildren.

To have experienced all this cataclysmic change, while caring selflessly for others in need, was no ordinary life. And like so many other women of her time, she nurtured a private desire that was always denied her. She wanted to be a writer. That was her real identity. But there was no opportunity. Until now. This is her collection of beautiful, simple poems and very funny short stories of a bygone age.

A SINGLE PETAL
Oliver Eade (ISBN 978-1-907203-42-8)

The very first winner of the national Local Legend Spiritual Writing Competition, this page-turner is a novel of murder, politics and passion set in ancient China. Yet its themes of loyalty, commitment and deep personal love are every bit as relevant for us today as they were in past times. The author is an expert on Chinese culture and history, and his debut adult novel deserves to become a classic.

5P1R1T R3V3L4T10N5
Nigel Peace (ISBN 978-1-907203-14-5)

With descriptions of more than a hundred proven prophetic dreams and many more everyday synchronicities, the author shows us that, without doubt, we can know the future and that everyone can receive genuine spiritual guidance for our lives' challenges. World-renowned biologist Dr Rupert Sheldrake has endorsed this book as "... vivid and fascinating ... pioneering research ..." and it was national runner-up in The People's Book Prize awards.

These titles are all available as paperbacks and eBooks.
Further details and extracts of these and many
other beautiful books may be seen at

www.local-legend.co.uk

www.ingramcontent.com/pod-product-compliance
Lightning Source LLC
Chambersburg PA
CBHW060352050426
42449CB00011B/2938